DK WORKBOOKS

pre-K Science

Author Hugh Westrup

Educational Consultant Kara Pranikoff

DK | Penguin Random House

US Editor Nancy Ellwood
US Educational Consultant Kara Pranikoff
Managing Art Editor Richard Czapnik
Senior Editors Fran Baines, Cécile Landau
Art Director Martin Wilson
Pre-production Francesca Wardell

DK Delhi
Asst. Editor Nishtha Kapil
Asst. Art Editors Tanvi Nathyal, Yamini Panwar
DTP Designer Anita Yadav
Dy. Managing Editor Soma B. Chowdhury

First American Edition, 2014
Published in the United States by DK Publishing
345 Hudson Street, New York, New York 10014

Copyright © 2014 Dorling Kindersley Limited
DK, a Division of Penguin Random House LLC
17 10 9 8 7 6 5 4 3 2
006-197329-01/14

A catalog record for this book
is available from the Library of Congress
ISBN: 978-1-4654-1726-8

DK books are available at special discounts when purchased in bulk
for sales promotions, premiums, fund-raising, or educational use.
For details, contact:
DK Publishing Special Markets
345 Hudson Street, New York, New York 10014
SpecialSales@dk.com.

Printed and bound in China

All images © Dorling Kindersley Limited
For further information see: www.dkimages.com

A WORLD OF IDEAS:
SEE ALL THERE IS TO KNOW

www.dk.com

Contents

This chart lists all the topics in the book.
Once you have completed each page,
stick a star in the correct box below.

Plants and animals are living things. They grow and change. They need food, air, and water to survive.

Circle the living things.

elephant

flowering plant

tricycle

dolphin

bird

teddy bear

Mammals are animals that have fur or hair.
Humans are mammals, too.

Point to each mammal and say its name out loud.

fox

cat

tortoise

groundhog

goose

monkey

Birds are animals that have feathers.
They also lay eggs.

Point to each animal that is a bird and say its name out loud.

penguin

peacock

robin

raccoon

bat

eagle

Fish are animals that live under water.
They have fins to help them swim.

Circle the animals that are fish.

seal

salmon

trout

tuna

shark

otter

Reptiles are land animals that have dry skin covered in scales. They also lay eggs.

Circle the animals that are reptiles.

alligator

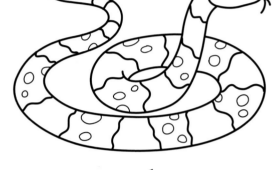

snake

squirrel

turtle

chickadee

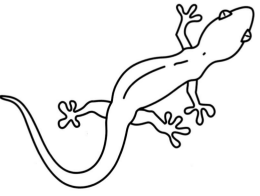

lizard

Amphibians are animals that live in water when they are young. When they are older, they live on land.

Circle the animals that are amphibians.

raccoon

frog

penguin

salamander

toad

beaver

Animals need homes just like people do. They need a place to protect them from their enemies and from the weather.

Draw a line between each animal and its home.

bear

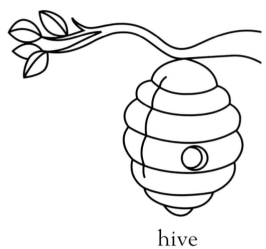

hive

bees

nest

bird

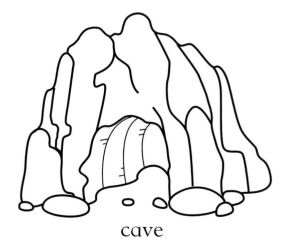

cave

Animals need food to survive.

What kind of animal is this?
Where does this animal live?

What food is the animal holding? Point to the food
it is holding and name it.

FACTS

Animals move around in different ways.

fly	hop	swim	walk

Touch each animal and say how it moves.

Can you move your body like one of the animals on this page?

Animals need to protect themselves from their enemies. Animals use different parts of their bodies to stay safe.

Draw a line to connect each animal to the part it uses to protect itself.

porcupine

claws, teeth

wasp

horn

rhinoceros

stinger

tiger

quills

People talk to share information. Animals communicate, or share information, by using special sounds.

Touch each animal and make the sound it makes.

Animals change as they get older.

Circle each baby animal. What is each baby animal called?

dog

puppy

duck

duckling

cat

kitten

sheep

lamb

A plant is a living thing. It needs light and water to survive. It is green and often grows in the ground. There are many kinds of plants.

| bush | cactus | flower | tree |

Can you find the picture of each plant?
Point to the picture of each plant.

Flowers come in many different shapes and colors.

Color the tulip orange. Color the sunflower yellow.
Color the daisy pink. Color the rose red.

daisy

tulip

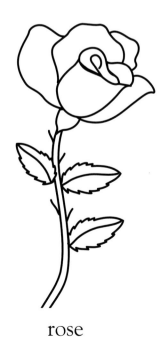

rose

sunflower

A leaf is a part of a plant that uses air and sunlight to make food. Leaves come in many different shapes.

Point to the leaf that is different in each row.

The part of the plant that holds the seeds is called the fruit. When seeds are planted in the ground they become new plants.

Point to the seeds in the fruit and color in each one.

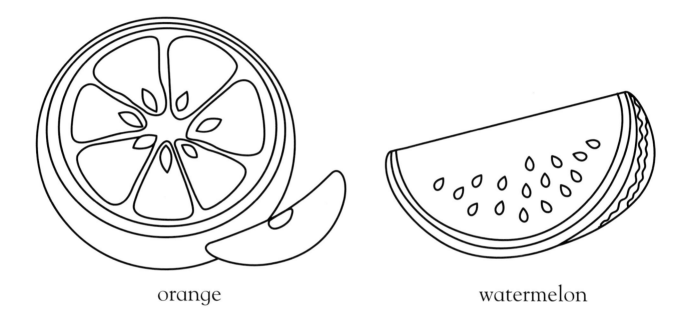

orange

watermelon

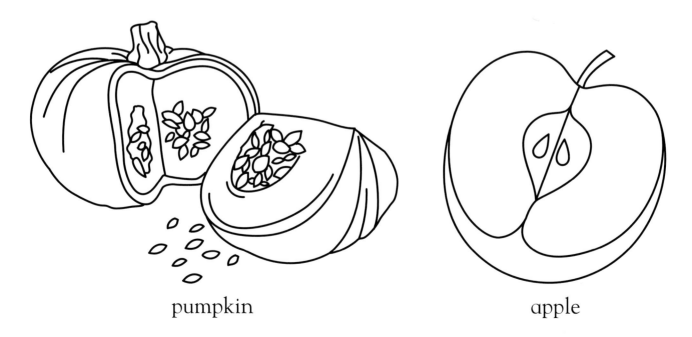

pumpkin

apple

★ Seed Growth

Seeds need water to grow.
As they grow they change.

TEST **What You Need:**

cotton balls   bean seeds   bowl of water   plastic bag

 What To Do:

1. Dip the cotton balls into water and place them in the bag. Use enough cotton balls to fill half the bag.

2. Place three or four beans in the cotton balls and close the bag.

3. Place the bag near a window and check it every day. If the cotton balls begin to get dry, add more water.

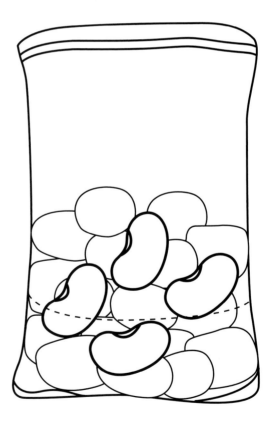

RESULT

After one week, the beans will sprout.

A plant changes as it grows.

The pictures show an apple tree growing. It starts as a seed and does not get its apples until it is fully grown. Put the stages of the apple tree in order by touching the picture that comes first, second, third, and fourth.

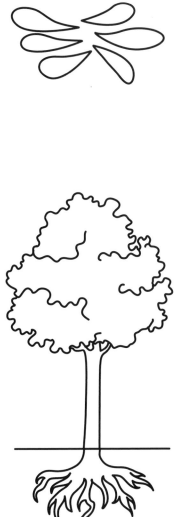

A farm is a place where a farmer grows plants and raises animals for food.

Touch each animal on the farm and say its name.
Then color in the picture.

Many animals live in the forest.

Touch each animal in the forest and say its name.
Then color in the picture.

FACTS

A lake is a body of fresh water. It is home to many plants and animals.

Circle the animals that you would find living in a lake.

duck	frog	dragonfly	fish

A desert is a very dry habitat. Many deserts are also very hot.

Circle the animals that you would find in a desert.

| coyote | rattlesnake | scorpion | vulture |

FACTS

Weather is what the air and sky are like each day.

Point to the picture that shows the strong wind blowing.
Touch the picture where it is raining.
Which picture shows lightning?
Point to the picture where it is snowing.

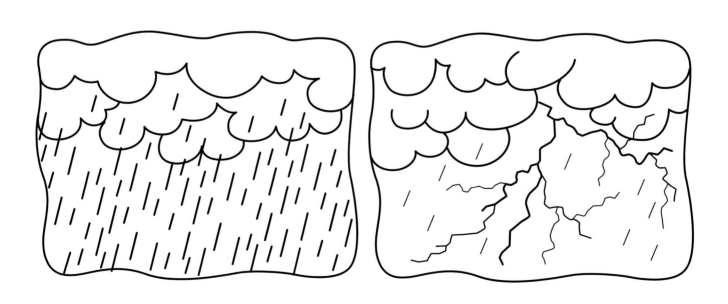

People wear different clothes for each type of weather.

Draw a line between each type of weather, and what you need for it.

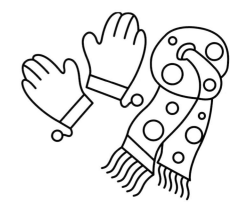

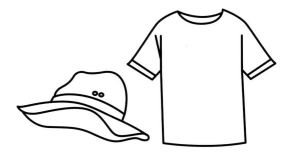

What other clothes do you have for different types of weather?

FACTS

Every year has four seasons. They are spring, summer, fall, and winter. The weather is different during each season.

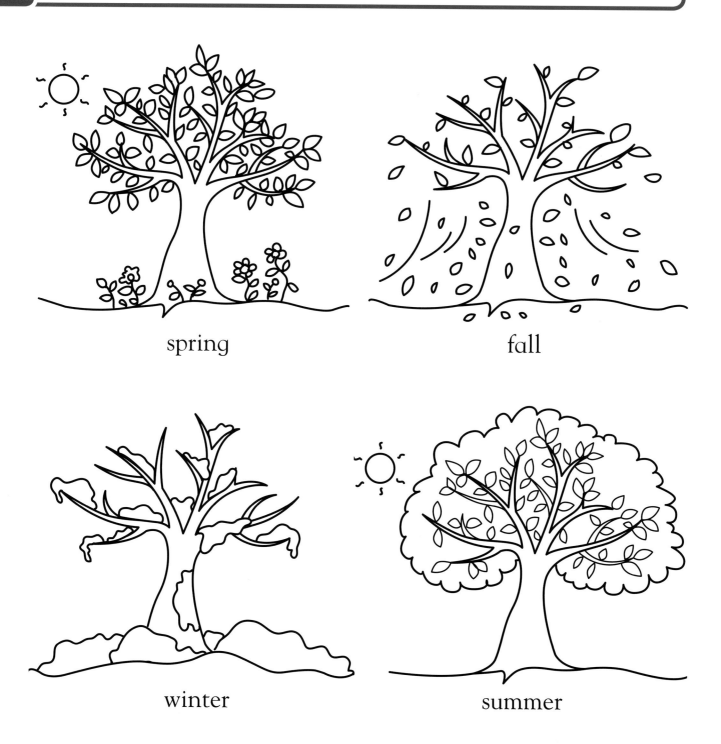

spring

fall

winter

summer

Which season is your favorite?

The human body has many parts.

Draw a line from each label to the correct body part.

chest
arm

head
foot

leg
hand

The senses help us learn about the world around us. There are five senses: hearing, sight, smell, taste, and touch.

| hearing | sight | smell | taste | touch |

Match the body part on the picture with the sense that it uses.

People change as they grow older.

These pictures show a person growing older. Touch the pictures from youngest (**1**) to oldest (**5**).

elderly person

5

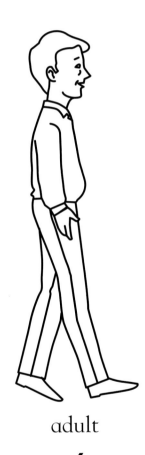

adult

4

child

2

teenager

3

baby

1

A family often has many members: children, parents, aunts, uncles, cousins, and grandparents.

Draw a picture of some of the people in your family.

Good food helps you to grow and stay healthy.

Circle the foods that are good for your health.

meat   fish   pasta   bread

milk   soft drinks   vegetables   rice

eggs   potato chips   candy   fruits

We do many things every day to stay healthy.

Touch each picture and name the activity the person is doing to stay healthy.

Which of these activities have you done today?

Some of the things in the world around us are solid.
Solids keep their shape. Other things are liquid.
Liquids flow freely.

Circle the things that are liquids.

milk

juice

sneakers

keys

cell phone

water

Water is the most common liquid on Earth.

Which of these activities is done with water?

What else do you like to do with water?

Objects that float stay on the surface of a liquid. Objects that sink fall to the bottom of a container of liquid.

Imagine that you put each of these objects into the bathtub. Touch each object and say if it would sink or float.

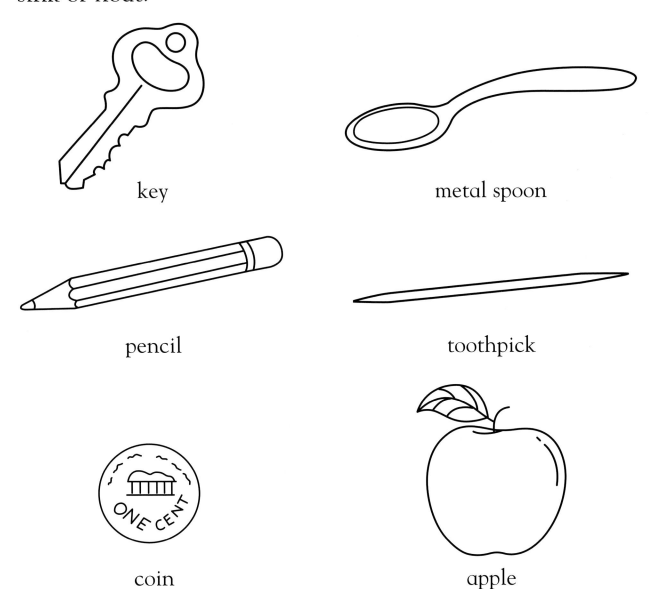

key

metal spoon

pencil

toothpick

coin

apple

A boat is a vehicle that floats on water.

TEST

What You Need:

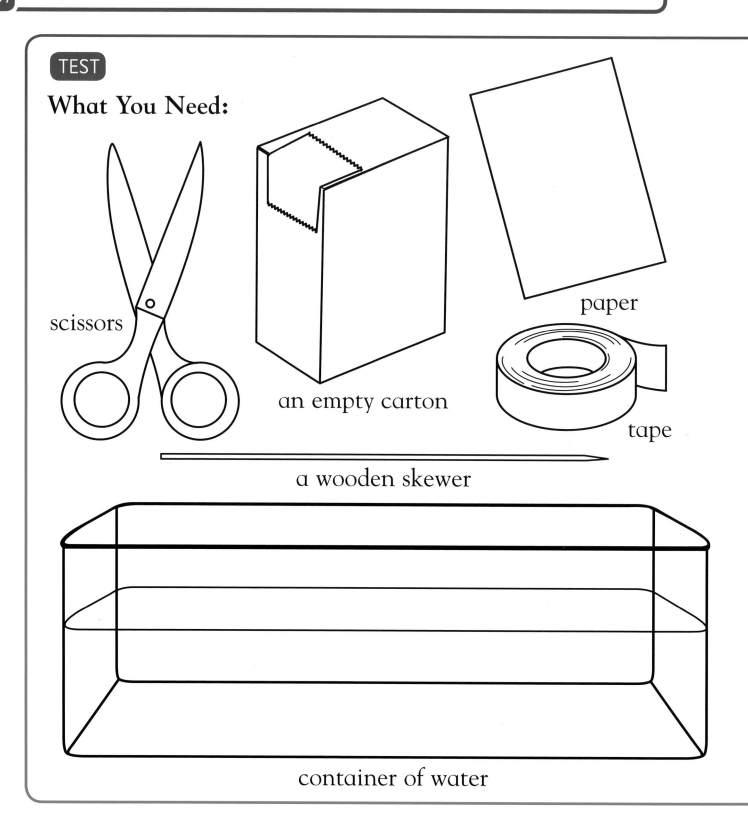

scissors

an empty carton

paper

tape

a wooden skewer

container of water

Float means to stay on the surface of water.

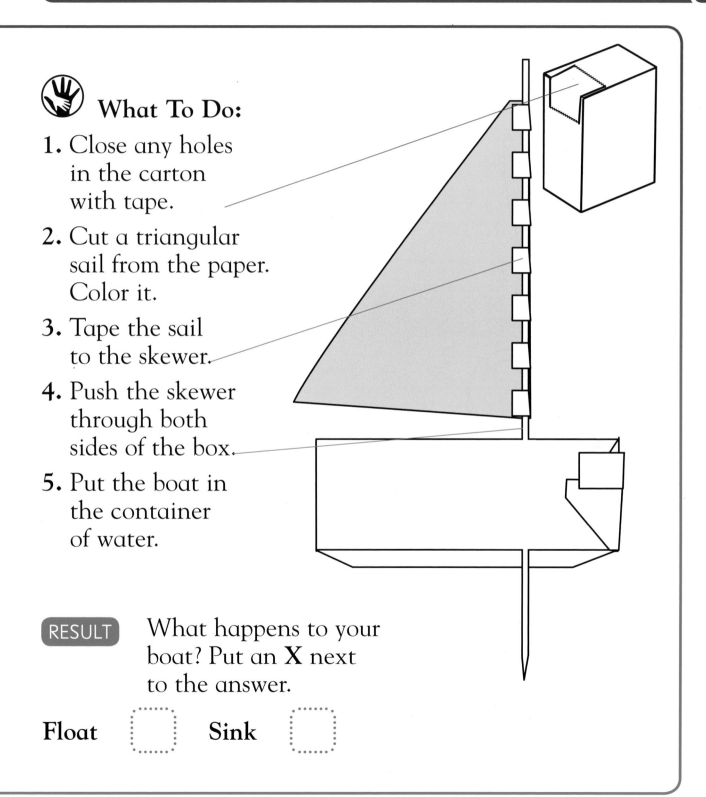

🖐 What To Do:

1. Close any holes in the carton with tape.

2. Cut a triangular sail from the paper. Color it.

3. Tape the sail to the skewer.

4. Push the skewer through both sides of the box.

5. Put the boat in the container of water.

RESULT What happens to your boat? Put an **X** next to the answer.

Float ☐   **Sink** ☐

A mixture is two or more things put together.

TEST

What You Need:

milk

grape juice

a clear glass

a spoon

 What To Do:

1. Pour some milk into the glass. What does it look like?

2. Now drink it. What does it taste like?

3. Add some grape juice. Stir with a spoon to mix.

RESULT

Color what you see.
What does it taste like?

Some liquids mix when they are put together.
Some liquids do not.

TEST

What You Need:

a clear
glass

3 tbsp
cooking oil

5 tbsp water mixed
with 2 drops of
blue food coloring

3 tbsp of
molasses

a spoon

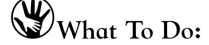 **What To Do:**

1. Pour the three liquids into the glass.

2. Stir well with the spoon.

3. Leave for one hour.

RESULT

Draw what you see.

FACTS

A solid can be mixed with a liquid.

TEST

What You Need:

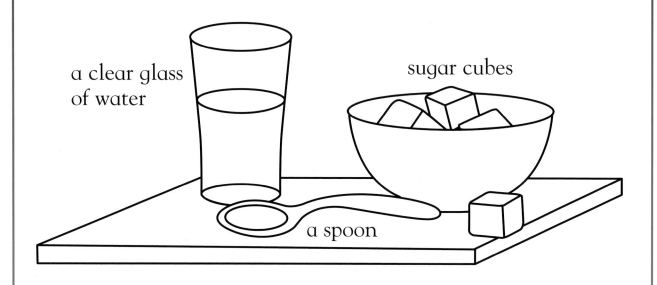

a clear glass of water

sugar cubes

a spoon

 What To Do:

1. Put a sugar cube into the water.
2. Stir well with the spoon.

RESULT

Put an **X** next to the picture that shows what happens.

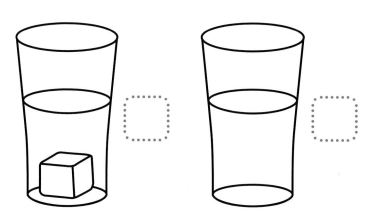

Two different solids can be mixed.

TEST

What You Need:

a clear mixing bowl

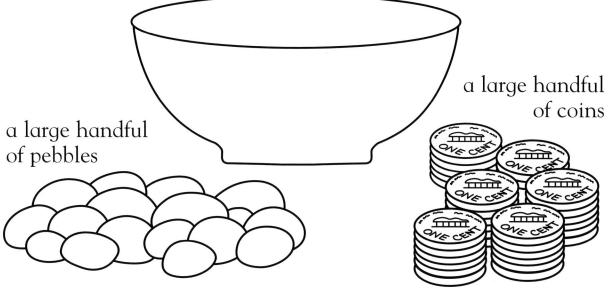

a large handful of coins

a large handful of pebbles

 What To Do:

1. Pour the coins and pebbles into the bowl.
2. Mix with your hands.

RESULT

What happens to the solids? Do they change or stay the same? Put an **X** next to the correct answer.

Change	
Stay the same	

FACTS

Sometimes a solid mixes with a liquid in a strange way.

TEST

What You Need:

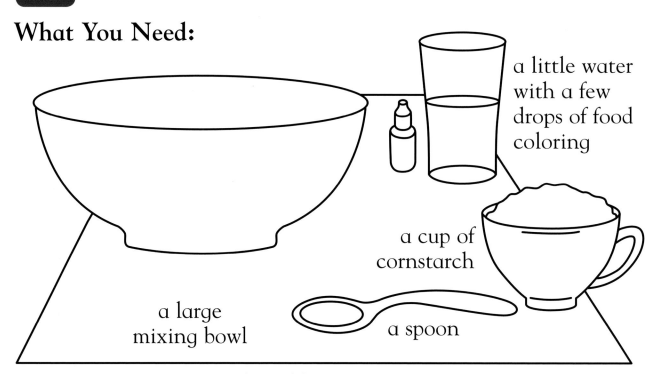

a little water with a few drops of food coloring

a cup of cornstarch

a large mixing bowl

a spoon

a newspaper to protect the table

 What To Do:

1. Pour the cornstarch into the bowl.
2. Add the colored water a little at a time and stir with a spoon.
3. Add water until the mixture is thick and gooey.

Play with the mixture:
- Stir it quickly and slowly.
- Squish it and squeeze it.
- Pull it.
- Roll it.
- Drop it.

Mixtures can be described by the way they act and feel.

RESULT How does the mixture feel as you play with it? Put an **X** next to the words on the chart.

Texture	
sticky as jelly	
rough as sandpaper	
smooth as paper	

Texture	
liquid like water	
solid like an ice cube	
hard as a rock	

FACTS

Red, blue, and yellow are primary colors.

Touch each object and say what color it is. Then color the objects.

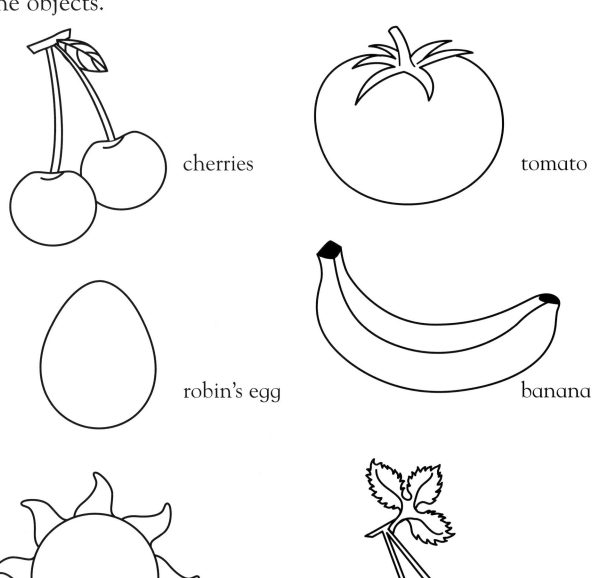

cherries

tomato

robin's egg

banana

sun

blueberries

What is your favorite color?

Mixing red, blue, and yellow creates new colors.

TEST

What You Need:

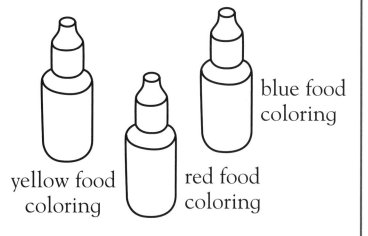

yellow food coloring

red food coloring

blue food coloring

3 plastic cups of water

 What To Do:

1. In one cup, add 3 yellow and 3 blue drops of coloring to the water.

2. In one cup, add 3 yellow and 3 red drops of coloring to the water.

3. In one cup, add 3 red and 3 blue drops of coloring to the water.

RESULT

Color the boxes.
What colors did you get?

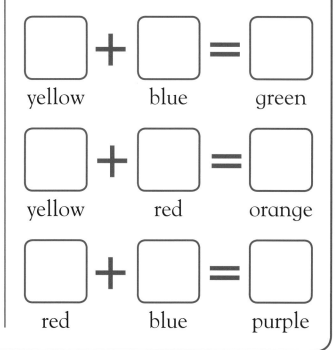

yellow	+	blue	=	green
yellow	+	red	=	orange
red	+	blue	=	purple

Certificate

Congratulations to

....

for successfully
finishing this book.

pre-K

GOOD JOB!

You're a star.

⭐ ⭐ ⭐ ⭐ ⭐

Date

....

Answer Section
with Parents' Notes

This book helps to support preschool children's understanding of science. This section provides explanatory notes, suggestions, and answers to all the science quizzes.

Contents

Working through this book, your child will gain knowledge about:

- living and nonliving things;
- animal classification;
- life cycles;
- food and shelter;
- plants;
- animal habitats;
- the human body;
- the senses;

- nutrition and hygiene;
- weather and the seasons;
- states of matter;
- motion;
- floating and sinking;
- mixtures;
- colors.

How to Help Your Child

Preschool children will not be able to read the instructions in this book—that is understood by the author. Therefore, there is an expectation that parents, guardians, or helpers will work closely with children as they progress through the book. Both parents/helpers and children can gain a great deal from working together.

Perhaps the most important thing you can do—both as you go through the workbook and in many everyday situations—is encourage children to be curious about the world around them. Whenever possible, ask them questions such as "Why?" and "What if?" Do not be negative about their answers, however silly they may seem. There is almost certainly a logic to your child's response, even if it is not correct. Explore and discuss their ideas with them.

Build your child's confidence with praise and encouragement. Celebrate their success.

★ Living Things

FACTS

Plants and animals are living things. They grow and change. They need food, air, and water to survive.

Circle the living things.

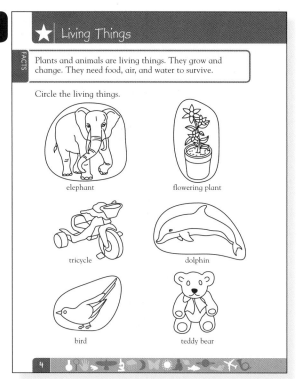

elephant

flowering plant

tricycle

dolphin

bird

teddy bear

Your child may identify something as being alive because it moves, and therefore may not realize that plants are also living things. You can extend this activity by looking at pictures in books, or by pointing out things in and outside the home, and asking your child, "Is this a living thing?"

Mammals ★

FACTS

Mammals are animals that have fur or hair. Humans are mammals, too.

Point to each mammal and say its name out loud.

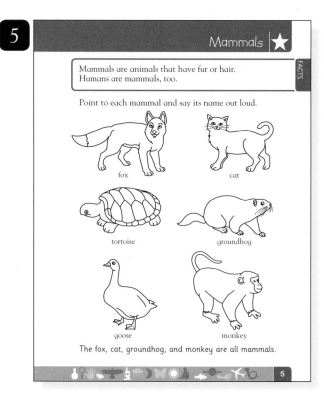

fox

cat

tortoise

groundhog

goose

monkey

The fox, cat, groundhog, and monkey are all mammals.

Scientists classify things—they sort them into groups with shared characteristics. Help your child to recognize one of the features of mammals—for instance, that they are covered in fur or hair. People are mammals, too. Discuss with your child other characteristics shared by mammals.

★ Birds

FACTS

Birds are animals that have feathers. They also lay eggs.

Point to each animal that is a bird and say its name out loud.

penguin

peacock

robin

raccoon

bat

eagle

The penguin, robin, peacock, and eagle are all birds.

Help your child to identify the characteristics that birds share: they have wings and feathers and they lay eggs. Point out that not all birds are able to fly, such as the penguin. Ask your child to think of other birds.

Fish ★

FACTS

Fish are animals that live under water. They have fins to help them swim.

Circle the animals that are fish.

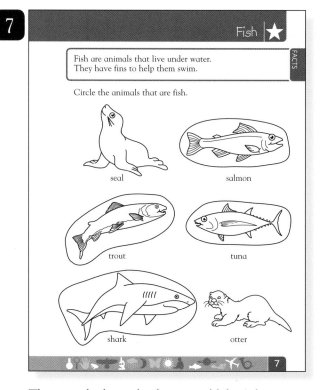

seal

salmon

trout

tuna

shark

otter

This page looks at the features of fish. Ask your child to name the different parts of fish: the fins, tail, and gills. Discuss together the differences and similarities between fish and sea mammals, such as how they breathe and swim.

★ Reptiles

FACTS

Reptiles are land animals that have dry skin covered in scales. They also lay eggs.

Circle the animals that are reptiles.

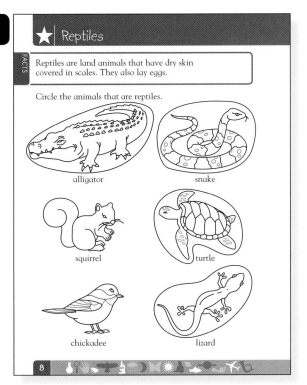

alligator

snake

squirrel

turtle

chickadee

lizard

Help your child to recognize the characteristics of reptiles. Point out that their scaly skin is dry and that they shed their outer skins as they grow. Although some reptiles, such as turtles, spend most of their lives in water, nearly all reptiles lay their eggs on land.

Amphibians ★

FACTS

Amphibians are animals that live in water when they are young. When they are older, they live on land.

Circle the animals that are amphibians.

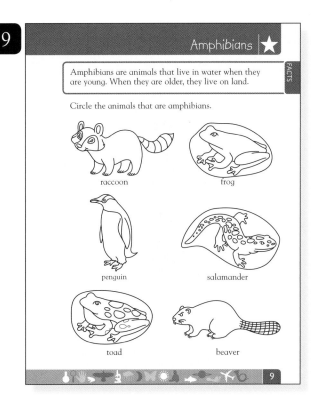

raccoon

frog

penguin

salamander

toad

beaver

This page focuses on amphibians. Discuss the life cycle of amphibians, and what the implications are of changing from life in the water to life on land.

★ Animal Homes

FACTS

Animals need homes just like people do. They need a place to protect them from their enemies and from the weather.

Draw a line between each animal and its home.

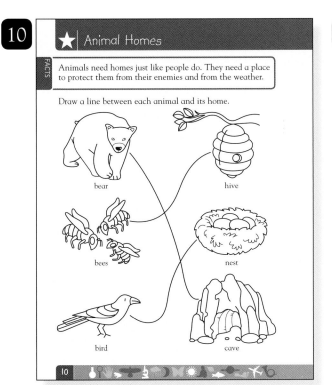

bear

hive

bees

nest

bird

cave

In this activity, your child matches animals with their homes. Talk together about the reasons animals need shelter, and how different homes suit their specific needs. Encourage your child to name other animal homes.

Animals Need Food ★

FACTS

Animals need food to survive.

What kind of animal is this?
Where does this animal live?

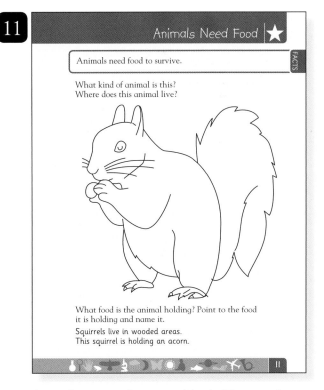

What food is the animal holding? Point to the food it is holding and name it.

Squirrels live in wooded areas.
This squirrel is holding an acorn.

Animals eat a wide range of foods. To expand on this activity, name other animals and ask your child to suggest what they eat. Talk about how the animal finds its food and how it eats—does the animal have sharp teeth, a long tongue, or a big beak, for example?

★ Animal Movement

FACTS

Animals move around in different ways.

| fly | hop | swim | walk |

Touch each animal and say how it moves.

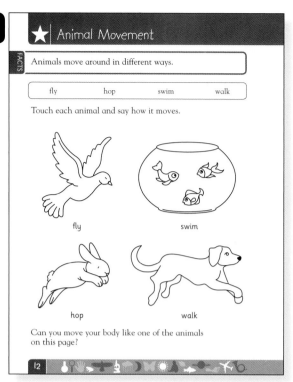

fly

swim

hop

walk

Can you move your body like one of the animals on this page?

This activity shows that animals move in different ways. Read out the names of the different forms of movement so your child can match each one to the correct animal. Encourage him or her to extend their vocabulary using words such as trot, gallop, leap, and soar.

Animal Protection ★

FACTS

Animals need to protect themselves from their enemies. Animals use different parts of their bodies to stay safe.

Draw a line to connect each animal to the part it uses to protect itself.

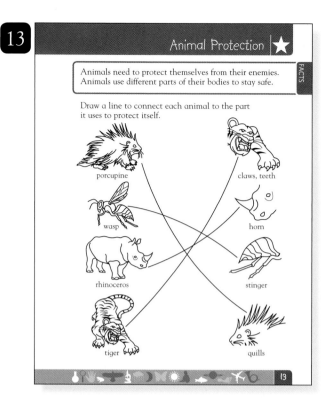

porcupine

claws, teeth

wasp

horn

rhinoceros

stinger

tiger

quills

By asking children to think about how certain features increase an animal's chances of survival, this page introduces the idea that animals adapt to their habitat. This activity focuses on self-defense.

★ Animal Sounds

FACTS

People talk to share information. Animals communicate, or share information, by using special sounds.

Touch each animal and make the sound it makes.

purr! meow!

cock-a-doodle-doo!

oink!

roar!

moo!

This page tests your child's observation of animal noises. To extend the activity, ask your child to suggest why animals make sounds. Possible answers are to attract mates, to warn other animals of danger, or tell other animals where to find food.

Young Animals ★

FACTS

Animals change as they get older.

Circle each baby animal. What is each baby animal called?

dog

duck

puppy

duckling

cat

sheep

kitten

lamb

This page introduces the idea that animals produce offspring. Encourage your child to use the correct vocabulary for the young animals. It is also fun to look at family photographs, for your child to see both how he or she looked as a baby, and observe that adult relatives were once young, too!

★ Plants

FACTS

A plant is a living thing. It needs light and water to survive. It is green and often grows in the ground. There are many kinds of plants.

| bush | cactus | flower | tree |

Can you find the picture of each plant?
Point to the picture of each plant.

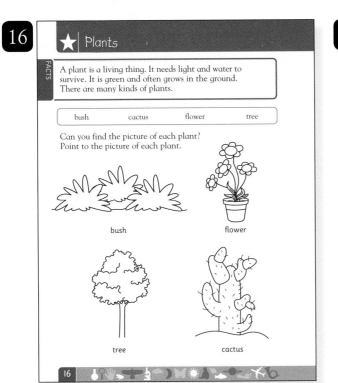

bush

flower

tree

cactus

This page requires your child to look carefully at the features of plants and to decide which one is a tree, bush, flower, or cactus. Ask your child why they gave the answer they did.

Flowers ★

FACTS

Flowers come in many different shapes and colors.

Color the tulip orange. Color the sunflower yellow.
Color the daisy pink. Color the rose red.

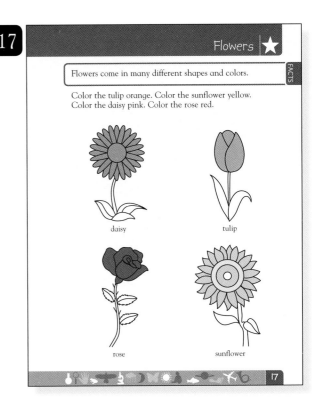

daisy

tulip

rose

sunflower

This coloring exercise encourages children to be aware of the different colors and shapes of flowers. When you go outside, encourage your child to spot flowers, look at their colors, and observe the very different shapes and patterns of their petals.

★ Leaves

FACTS

A leaf is a part of a plant that uses air and sunlight to make food. Leaves come in many different shapes.

Point to the leaf that is different in each row.

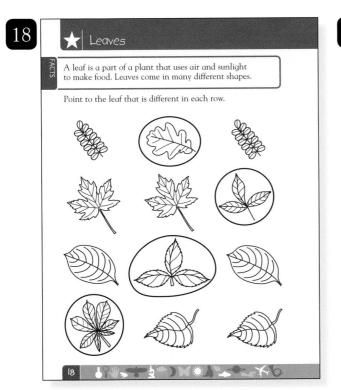

Different plants have different leaves, and this page requires your child to look closely at their shapes. In the fall, it is fun to extend this exercise by collecting leaves of different colors and shapes. Your child can then observe, measure, and sort the leaves they have collected.

Seeds ★

FACTS

The part of the plant that holds the seeds is called the fruit. When seeds are planted in the ground they become new plants.

Point to the seeds in the fruit and color in each one.

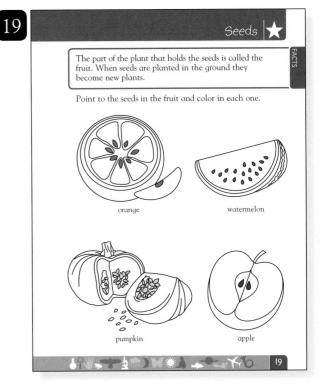

orange

watermelon

pumpkin

apple

This exercise focuses on the seeds of fruit. Explain to your child that it is from these seeds that new plants will grow. Look at fruits you have at home, and ask your child to identify the seeds. You can also plant some of the seeds together.

★ Seed Growth

Seeds need water to grow.
As they grow they change.

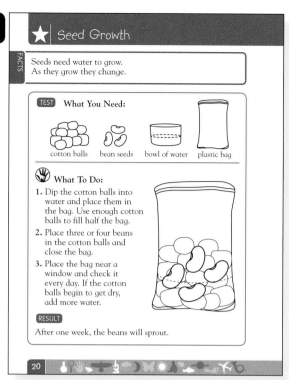

TEST **What You Need:**

cotton balls   bean seeds   bowl of water   plastic bag

What To Do:

1. Dip the cotton balls into water and place them in the bag. Use enough cotton balls to fill half the bag.
2. Place three or four beans in the cotton balls and close the bag.
3. Place the bag near a window and check it every day. If the cotton balls begin to get dry, add more water.

RESULT

After one week, the beans will sprout.

This activity allows children to observe how seeds change as they grow. As the bean grows, point out the difference between the shoot and the roots. Make sure not to let the beans dry out, and you will soon see the first leaves sprout.

Life Cycle of a Plant ★

A plant changes as it grows.

The pictures show an apple tree growing. It starts as a seed and does not get its apples until it is fully grown. Put the stages of the apple tree in order by touching the picture that comes first, second, third, and fourth.

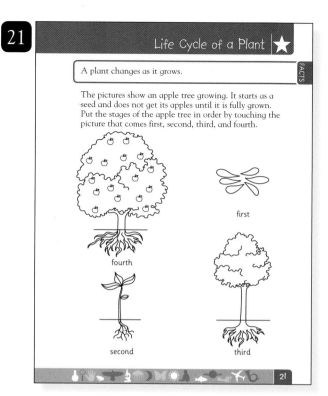

first

fourth

second

third

This page tests your child's understanding of the life cycle of a plant. Start by talking together about exactly what each picture shows, then ask your child to put the pictures in sequence. Discuss how the tree is changing: for example, note how the roots extend and the stem grows thicker.

★ Farm

A farm is a place where a farmer grows plants and raises animals for food.

Touch each animal on the farm and say its name. Then color in the picture.

The animals shown on the farm are horse, cow, pig, and rooster.

Encourage your child to tell you what they know about life on the farm—why the farmer keeps certain animals, what the animals produce, and how the farmer cares for them. You can also discuss different crops that a farmer would grow and the seasons for planting and harvesting.

Forest ★

Many animals live in the forest.

Touch each animal in the forest and say its name. Then color in the picture.

The animals shown in the forest are squirrel, deer, racoon, bear, and bird.

Here the focus is on life in the forest. The goal of this exercise is to help your child understand the relationship between a habitat and the creatures that live there. Discuss the features of a forest in more detail with your child, such as how the trees provide food and shelter for the animals.

★ Lake

FACTS A lake is a body of fresh water. It is home to many plants and animals.

Circle the animals that you would find living in a lake.

| duck | frog | dragonfly | fish |

This page looks at the habitat of a lake. Talk more about the animals in the picture and how they live and feed in the lake. What types of animal are they—mammals, birds, amphibians, or reptiles?

Desert ★

FACTS A desert is a very dry habitat. Many deserts are also very hot.

Circle the animals that you would find in a desert.

| coyote | rattlesnake | scorpion | vulture |

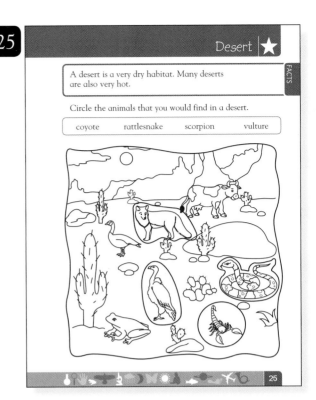

A desert is an extreme habitat. Talk with your child about the very dry conditions, and how that means there is little vegetation and few animals. The plants and animals that do live in a desert have special features to help them survive there.

★ Weather

FACTS Weather is what the air and sky are like each day.

Point to the picture that shows the strong wind blowing.
Touch the picture where it is raining.
Which picture shows lightning?
Point to the picture where it is snowing.

wind

snow

rain

lightning

The weather is a good topic when you want to explain the forces in the world. To help your child identify the type of weather shown in each picture, talk in more detail about the scenes, such as the lightning, clouds, and wind in the trees.

Outerwear ★

FACTS People wear different clothes for each type of weather.

Draw a line between each type of weather, and what you need for it.

What other clothes do you have for different types of weather?

This activity emphasizes the impact of the weather on all of our lives, including the way we dress. It also highlights the idea that the weather is always changing, and it can be wet or dry, hot or cold outside. Ask your child to describe how they feel about the different types of weather shown on the page.

★ The Seasons

FACTS Every year has four seasons. They are spring, summer, fall, and winter. The weather is different during each season.

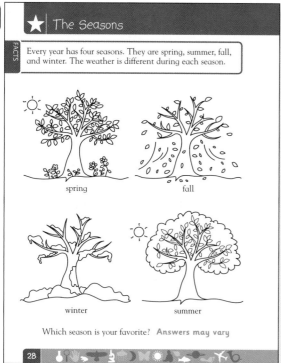

spring

fall

winter

summer

Which season is your favorite? **Answers may vary**

Before you begin this activity, go over the names of the different seasons and their sequence with your child. To help your child identify which season is which, discuss each picture together and guide them toward the details of the scenes.

The Human Body ★

The human body has many parts. FACTS

Draw a line from each label to the correct body part.

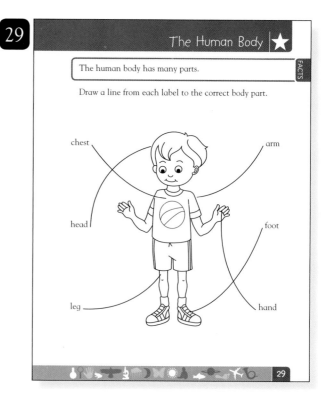

chest

arm

head

foot

leg

hand

On this page, your child practices naming parts of the human body using the correct vocabulary. Extend this exercise by playing a game in which you call out the names of a body part and your child has to point to it on their own body.

★ The Senses

FACTS The senses help us learn about the world around us. There are five senses: hearing, sight, smell, taste, and touch.

| hearing | sight | smell | taste | touch |

Match the body part on the picture with the sense that it uses.

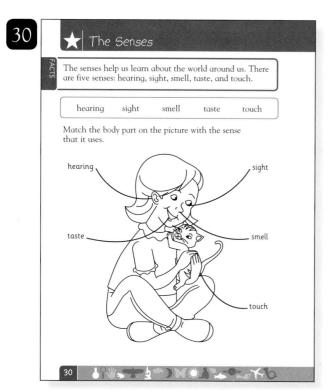

hearing

sight

taste

smell

touch

This exercise identifies the five senses and links them to the correct parts of the body. Discuss with your child why the senses are important—that they tell you what is happening in the world around you.

Growing Up ★

People change as they grow older. FACTS

These pictures show a person growing older. Touch the pictures from youngest (**1**) to oldest (**5**).

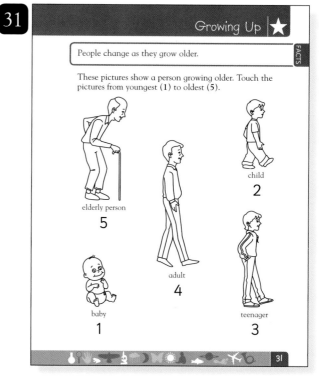

elderly person
5

child
2

adult
4

teenager
3

baby
1

Humans grow and change throughout life. Discuss characteristics that indicate age, such as height, hair color, and skin appearance. Ask your child to link family members and friends to the different stages shown.

★ My Family

FACTS A family often has many members: children, parents, aunts, uncles, cousins, and grandparents.

Draw a picture of some of the people in your family.
Drawings may vary

There are many ways to be a family. This activity mentions various family members. Discuss, too, the relationship between members of your extended family. For example, does your child understand that their uncle is your brother?

Good Food ★

FACTS Good food helps you to grow and stay healthy.

Circle the foods that are good for your health.

meat   fish   pasta   bread

milk   soft drinks   vegetables   rice

eggs   potato chips   candy   fruits

Talk about each of the foods shown in the picture with your child and discuss what makes those foods good for them. Explain, too, why some foods should only be eaten in small amounts.

★ Healthy Habits

FACTS We do many things every day to stay healthy.

Touch each picture and name the activity the person is doing to stay healthy.

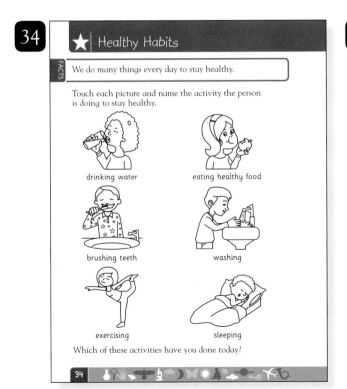

drinking water   eating healthy food

brushing teeth   washing

exercising   sleeping

Which of these activities have you done today?

This page reinforces the importance of healthy eating and good hygiene. Use the pictures to discuss the impact that eating healthy food, drinking enough water, getting enough sleep, and exercising have on growth, energy, and health. Good hygiene helps protect us from germs.

Solids and Liquids ★

FACTS Some of the things in the world around us are solid. Solids keep their shape. Other things are liquid. Liquids flow freely.

Circle the things that are liquids.

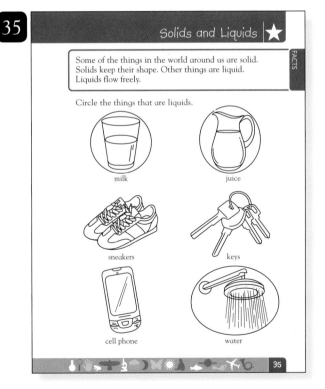

milk   juice

sneakers   keys

cell phone   water

Children learn in science that everything is made of matter and that matter exists in different states. Understanding the different characteristics of liquids and solids is the first step. To extend this activity, find other objects around the home and ask your child if they are a liquid or a solid.

★ Water

Water is the most common liquid on Earth.

Which of these activities is done with water?

Watering plants, washing, and swimming are done with water.
What else do you like to do with water? **Answers may vary**

Water is the most important liquid on Earth and is studied in all branches of science. Life cannot exist without water. Illustrate this point by talking to your child about the many ways they use water daily. Think, too, about water in the wider world—in lakes, oceans, and as an element of weather.

Floating and Sinking ★

Objects that float stay on the surface of a liquid. Objects that sink fall to the bottom of a container of liquid.

Imagine that you put each of these objects into the bathtub. Touch each object and say if it would sink or float.

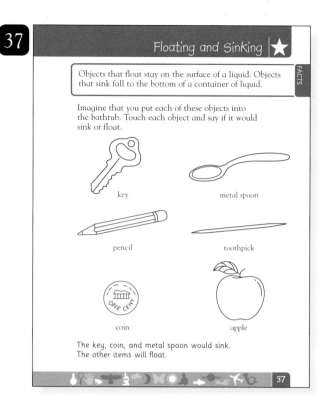

key

metal spoon

pencil

toothpick

coin

apple

The key, coin, and metal spoon would sink.
The other items will float.

The purpose of this activity is to help your child understand the concept that certain items float. Start by talking about things that float and things that do not float.

★ Build a Boat

A boat is a vehicle that floats on water.

TEST

What You Need:

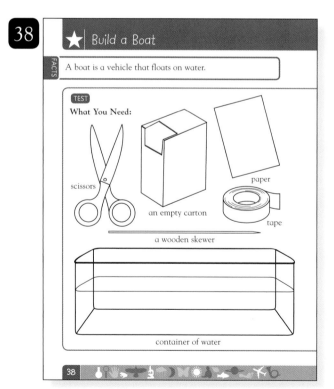

scissors

an empty carton

paper

tape

a wooden skewer

container of water

This practical activity is a fun way to explore floating further. Making and playing with the model boat will give your child an idea of the qualities of buoyancy.

Build a Boat ★

Float means to stay on the surface of water.

✋ **What To Do:**

1. Close any holes in the carton with tape.
2. Cut a triangular sail from the paper. Color it.
3. Tape the sail to the skewer.
4. Push the skewer through both sides of the box.
5. Put the boat in the container of water.

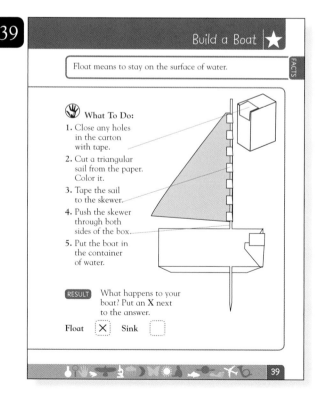

RESULT What happens to your boat? Put an **X** next to the answer.

Float [X] Sink [ ]

For a further activity, add small objects to the boat, such as plastic figurines, to see how this affects buoyancy.

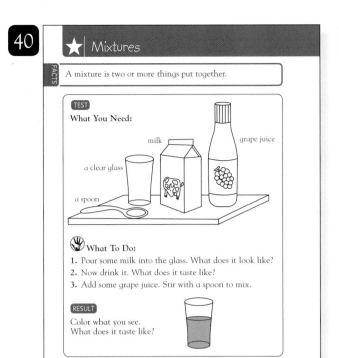

★ | Mixtures

FACTS

A mixture is two or more things put together.

TEST

What You Need:

milk

grape juice

a clear glass

a spoon

✋ What To Do:

1. Pour some milk into the glass. What does it look like?
2. Now drink it. What does it taste like?
3. Add some grape juice. Stir with a spoon to mix.

RESULT

Color what you see.
What does it taste like?

This page introduces children to the idea of experimentation by measuring, testing, and observing. Here your child explores what happens when you mix two liquids. Encourage them to predict the results of the experiment.

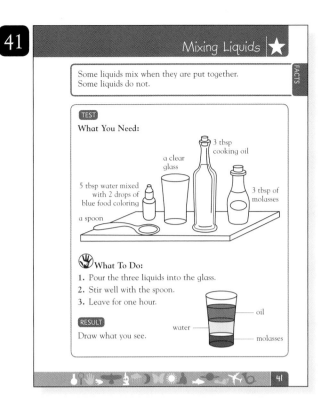

Mixing Liquids | ★

FACTS

Some liquids mix when they are put together.
Some liquids do not.

TEST

What You Need:

3 tbsp cooking oil

a clear glass

5 tbsp water mixed with 2 drops of blue food coloring

3 tbsp of molasses

a spoon

✋ What To Do:

1. Pour the three liquids into the glass.
2. Stir well with the spoon.
3. Leave for one hour.

RESULT

Draw what you see.

oil

water

molasses

This activity builds on the previous experiment, mixing three different liquids that behave very differently. Observe the characteristics of each liquid before you mix them together. Again, ask your child to predict the results, and discuss the outcome together.

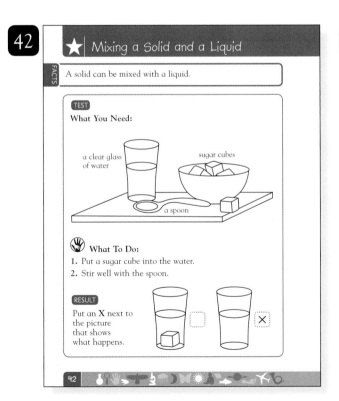

★ | Mixing a Solid and a Liquid

FACTS

A solid can be mixed with a liquid.

TEST

What You Need:

a clear glass of water

sugar cubes

a spoon

✋ What To Do:

1. Put a sugar cube into the water.
2. Stir well with the spoon.

RESULT

Put an **X** next to the picture that shows what happens.

Make sure that your child understands that they are mixing things in two different states of matter—a solid and a liquid. Ask them to predict what will happen. You can extend this activity by experimenting with other solids such as flour, salt, and baking soda.

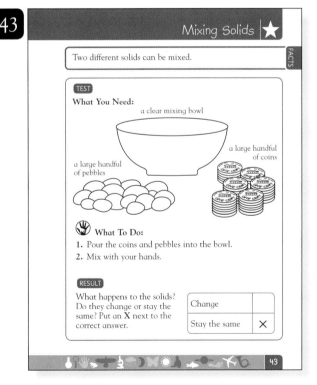

Mixing Solids | ★

FACTS

Two different solids can be mixed.

TEST

What You Need:

a clear mixing bowl

a large handful of coins

a large handful of pebbles

✋ What To Do:

1. Pour the coins and pebbles into the bowl.
2. Mix with your hands.

RESULT

What happens to the solids? Do they change or stay the same? Put an **X** next to the correct answer.

Change	
Stay the same	×

This page explores the mixing of solids. Ask your child to predict what will happen, and to compare and contrast these results with those of all the mixing experiments with liquids.

★ Weird Mixtures

FACTS Sometimes a solid mixes with a liquid in a strange way.

TEST

What You Need:

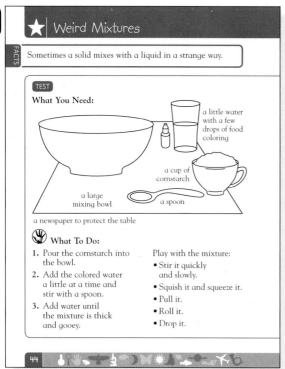

a little water with a few drops of food coloring

a cup of cornstarch

a large mixing bowl

a spoon

a newspaper to protect the table

What To Do:

1. Pour the cornstarch into the bowl.
2. Add the colored water a little at a time and stir with a spoon.
3. Add water until the mixture is thick and gooey.

Play with the mixture:
- Stir it quickly and slowly.
- Squish it and squeeze it.
- Pull it.
- Roll it.
- Drop it.

This is a fun activity because cornstarch behaves in such an unexpected way—sometimes like a liquid, sometimes like a solid.

Weird Mixtures ★

FACTS Mixtures can be described by the way they act and feel.

RESULT How does the mixture feel as you play with it? Put an **X** next to the words on the chart.
Answers may vary

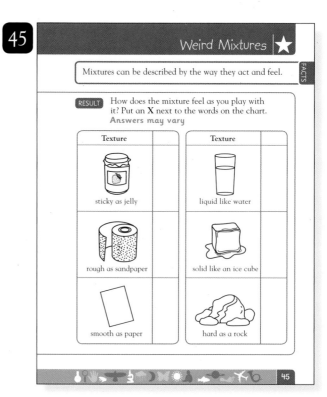

Texture	Texture
sticky as jelly	liquid like water
rough as sandpaper	solid like an ice cube
smooth as paper	hard as a rock

Give your child plenty of opportunity to play with and observe the mixture that is created, and ask the question: "Is it a liquid or a solid?"

★ Primary Colors

FACTS Red, blue, and yellow are primary colors.

Touch each object and say what color it is. Then color the objects.

cherries

tomato

robin's egg

banana

sun

blueberries

What is your favorite color? **Answers may vary**

This page introduces the primary colors. Extend this activity by asking your child to spot these colors in the world around them, both at home and outdoors.

Mixing Primary Colors ★

FACTS Mixing red, blue, and yellow creates new colors.

TEST

What You Need:

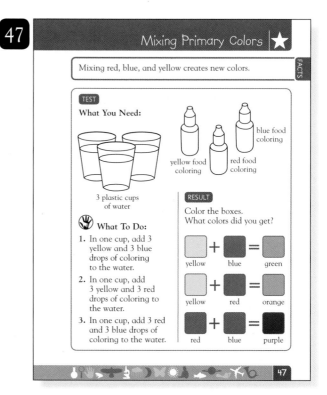

blue food coloring

yellow food coloring

red food coloring

3 plastic cups of water

What To Do:

1. In one cup, add 3 yellow and 3 blue drops of coloring to the water.
2. In one cup, add 3 yellow and 3 red drops of coloring to the water.
3. In one cup, add 3 red and 3 blue drops of coloring to the water.

RESULT

Color the boxes. What colors did you get?

yellow + blue = green

yellow + red = orange

red + blue = purple

This experiment is a fun way to demonstrate that primary colors are the building blocks of all other colors. Food coloring can be messy and stain permanently, so cover all surfaces with a layer of newspaper and make sure that your child is wearing an apron to protect their clothing.